*A Breeze Called the Fremantle Doctor*

# Other Books by Sonia Gernes

*Brief Lives*  (Poems)
*Women at Forty*  (Poems)
*The Way to St. Ives*  (Novel)

# A Breeze Called the Fremantle Doctor

Poem / Tales by

## SONIA GERNES

*For John on his birthday — with fond memories and all best wishes.*

*Sonia*

University of Notre Dame Press
Notre Dame, Indiana

*april 1998*

Published by
The University of Notre Dame Press
Notre Dame, Indiana 46556
All Rights Reserved

Designed by Wendy McMillen and Jeannette Morgenroth
Set in 11/14 Aldus by The Book Page, Inc.
Printed in the U. S. A. by Braun-Brumfield, Inc.

Grateful acknowledgment is made to the editors of the
following publications where some of these
poems first appeared: *Argo, Bits, Poetry Northwest,*
*Seattle Review.*
Copyright 1981 by Sonia Gernes

*Library of Congress Cataloging-in-Publication Data*

Gernes, Sonia.
    A breeze called the fremantle doctor : poem/tales /
Sonia Gernes.
        p.   cm.
    ISBN 0-268-02150-3 (alk. paper)
    1. Frontier and pioneer life—Minnesota—Poetry.
2. Women—Minnesota—Poetry.   I. Title.
PS3557.E685B67   1997
811'.54—dc21                                    97-15583
                                                         CIP

∞ *The paper used in this publication meets the minimum*
*requirements of the American National Standard for*
*Information Sciences—Permanence of Paper for Printed*
*Library Materials, ANSI Z39.48-1984.*

# Contents

# Acknowledgments

The author wishes to thank the following for their aid in bringing this volume to publication:

The Fremantle City Library for permission to use print 1723, the Battye Library of the Western Australian Museum for permission to use print 1043B/32, and the Fremantle Museum and Art Centre for their assistance.

The Pipestone (Minnesota) County Historical Museum for access to their archives.

The Institute for Scholarship in the Liberal Arts at the University of Notre Dame for travel funds to visit the Pipestone archives.

The late Laura Grover, who first published "The Mutes of Sleepy Eye" in a limited chapbook edition.

The help, encouragement, and feedback of Naomi Meara, Philippa Ryan, Adam Fortunate Eagle, Carole Walton, Joan McIntosh, Max Westler, Julie Herrick White, and my faithful editor, Ann Rice.

I am indebted to many sources for the Native American legends and stories that appear in "The Indian School," in particular, *Legends of the Lakota* by James LaPointe.

## Author's Note

The places used as settings for these poems are real: the Pipestone Indian Training School, the town of Sleepy Eye, Minnesota, and the Lunatic Asylum (later Ladies Residence and currently Art Centre) of Fremantle, Western Australia. The events, however, are fictional, as are the characters, who exist only in the love the author bears them.

All photos in the Indian School section are from the scrapbooks of Sophia Boerboom Gernes. The photos in the Sleepy Eye section were taken by the author.

# Preface

These poems tell their own stories. Each has speakers whose voices are not my own. But in back of every story is another story, and as a teller of tales, I am sometimes asked for those stories too. So for Ann and Marge and Jeannette, who asked, I give three little tales in prose. Other readers may ignore them or not, but all of these tales are true.

## 1. Pipestone

 I began to search for my mother when she had almost disappeared. "Here, you take these," she said, thrusting a box of jumbled scrapbooks and photo albums at me the summer my father's stroke convinced her to move from the farmhouse to an apartment near his nursing home. I was back in Minnesota to help her get organized, to get rid of the effluvium of eighty years so that my siblings would have an easier time with the actual move. In this mission, I failed entirely. She would throw away nothing. She would take a dusty piece of driftwood stuck

with plastic flowers from a cupboard shelf, muse about which of her friends might have made it, and then put it back while I held a garbage bag open and empty.

Now and then she would offer me things: a mildewed picnic basket, a cookie jar missing its lid. Putting them in my car seemed the only way to get rid of anything, and I'm enough of a family historian to want the photos and scrapbooks preserved. But I didn't make much of them; I glanced through and put them in my attic when I got home. Meanwhile, things worsened. My mother hated the apartment, hated living alone, became so erratic mentally that we weren't surprised by the diagnosis we feared: Alzheimer's, advancing its inexorable march through her brain cells. Now the farm had to be sold to pay for both their care, and from the depths of a closet emerged a box of letters I never knew existed—a lot of letters, three years worth of weekly data and dreaming between a young couple deterred from marriage by the Great Depression, a young couple who weren't my parents yet. "She said she wants you to have them," my brother said, presenting me with the carton. "I think she hopes you'll write something."

I wasn't thrilled by the implied assignment. My mother's usual response to my writing had been to say, "Well, that's very nice, honey," and then to tell me everything about the piece that was factually wrong. My mother was usually sure of what was right. She was the most educated woman in our farm community, and in my young eyes, the most powerful. She knew everything: the recipe for lye soap, how to make bound buttonholes, which magazines were wholesome enough for children to read, and why it was silly to fear public speaking. She was the neighborhood arbiter, adviser, organist, barber, and reference desk, and at times I resented it. At times I stayed in my room with pencil and paper and created worlds she couldn't critique.

Now this most competent of women had no power at all, and I was having trouble dealing with that. While she forgot where I lived and what I did, I spent the long evenings of a summer reading letters by a young woman who was surprisingly tentative, dependent on her father's advice, giddy with her first teaching success. As she forgot my name and how to tie her shoes, I poured over scrapbooks and albums, urgent to construct a woman who would not be my mother for a dozen years.

I say "construct" deliberately. Even letters are ruled by the prevailing discourse of the time, and these were bulky with slang and chitchat about mutual friends, coy about admitting love, nearly silent about major events: their engagement, her father's death. The scraps and fragments I found most intriguing were those from the year she taught at the Pipestone Indian Training School, perhaps because she'd seemed so proud of that experience, perhaps because in later years she kept reminding me that she could have been a career woman too.

I made a trip to Pipestone the next summer. I walked the trail through the quarry to Winniwissa Falls, brought back samples of the flesh-red stone used for centuries of peace pipes, and waded through the archives of the historical museum. I didn't find my mother anywhere at all, but I realized I really didn't need to find her. We select our memories, consciously or not. We weave the tales that explain to ourselves our lives. My mother knew I was a creature given to invention when she consigned the letters to my keeping. At some level, she must also have known I'd use those hints and scraps to construct the woman and the tale I most needed to hear.

## 2. Sleepy Eye

One morning in graduate school, between my written and oral doctoral exams, I woke up, got out of bed, and fell over. My equilibrium was gone, my left ear rang, and either the floor or my stomach was lurching. I made it to the bathroom by clutching the wall, then crawled back under the covers and spent the day lying very still. The next day I could walk again, so I presented myself to the student health center. They said a cold had gone into my Eustachian tube. I said I didn't have a cold. They said I hadn't noticed. Three days later we had the same exchange. Three *weeks* later, they referred me to the Ear Clinic at the University Hospital.

The doctors there were quite pleased to see me; I presented a genuine mystery for their med students to solve. I had most of the symptoms of Ménière's disease and verifiable nerve damage, but I tested negative on every diagnostic procedure (most of them unpleasant) that they ran. A freak virus, they finally decided—a 20 percent hearing loss and tinnitus, both of them permanent but not progressive. Okay, I thought, I'll try to live with that, but they were wrong.

As I slogged through my dissertation, the hearing loss worsened. The tinnitus, at inopportune moments, would start roaring or change in pitch. For days at a time I experienced not exactly dizziness or vertigo, but vague nausea, a hung-over sense that the world was slightly out of kilter, everything off by half an inch. Finally, the chief-of-staff sat me down. (I'd been bumped up through the ranks as I baffled each succeeding layer of expertise.) He said they were sorry. He said there were no more tests anyone could run. He said if the vertigo got so bad I couldn't work, they could try surgery, but it probably wouldn't do any good. He said there was no treatment. He said medical science, after all, can't solve everything.

I went home and wept. I thought my life was ruined. (It wasn't, of course, though my left ear has kept me out of bars and made large parties a serious strain.) I knew I faced a future of saying "Pardon? Could you repeat that?" and jostling to aim my good ear, but it was worse than that: I faced a lifetime of fearing that any morning I could wake to find my good ear mysteriously destroying its own nerve endings.

That's why I became interested in the problems of the deaf, why years later in South Bend, Indiana, I agreed to be part of an Arts Council project to bring poetry to the deaf. In truth, I thought the whole thing was a little flakey, but I wanted to show my goodwill, so with an American Sign Language interpreter, I showed up to teach a roomful of people how to use their language to make poetry. I was in for a surprise: their language *is* poetry! It's based on metaphor and symbol to a degree that no spoken language is. My roomful of pupils didn't seem to think this was a flakey project. Their hands traced and fluttered and smacked as memories and insights and longing took shape in the air. At the conclusion of the project, a sign poet from the National Theatre of the Deaf came to do a poetry reading with an English translator. In her hands, weather changed before our eyes, telephone wires hummed their way into the distance, hearts broke and mended. I could hardly breathe; it was the most exhilarating poetry reading I've ever heard or seen.

Back home that night, I was too energized to sleep. I began thinking of Clara, a woman in my signed poetry class, who wrote a poem about a barn that burned in her childhood in the thirties. I started wondering what childhood had been like for Clara: Did she have hearing siblings? Did she have deaf friends? Was she sent away to school? I pictured a little girl in brown cotton stockings, boarding a train with a note pinned to her coat to name her destination. I began to remember my own train journeys across Minnesota as a small child—how I cracked up every time the conductor came through the car calling out: *Mankato, New Ulm, Sleepy Eye . . .* Sleepy Eye. It was the funniest name in the world.

Suddenly I was out of bed, turning on the typewriter. Clara, a little deaf girl from Sleepy Eye was getting on a train with that note pinned to her coat. She was going to the State School in Faribault, but she was doing this in memory because she was grown now; she was a widow in her fifties, thinking about the different ways deafness affected each generation. Were her children deaf? No, but other children were—children who had grown up in Sleepy Eye—edgy children who were trying to work out their own private quarrels with the hearing world.

When I went back to bed that night, there were three mutes in Sleepy Eye, and just offstage were the people their deafness unsettled—the ones with two good ears and quick-triggered tongues, the ones whose ability to hear was, nevertheless, impaired.

## 3. Fremantle

I went to Western Australia in 1993 because I couldn't think of a good reason not to go. I had the requisite experience to work with university students in a foreign setting, and a change of climate might be good for a crippling headache syndrome brought on by the approach of menopause. So when I was asked to go to a new study-abroad program in Fremantle with twenty-five Notre Dame students, I said yes, but with misgivings. The Perth/Fremantle area stands in isolation on the western edge of the map, a dot in a vast emptiness, and I didn't know if I could handle the heat.

Nighttimes weren't too bad. The ocean breeze the Aussies call "the doctor" did, as advertised, come in most afternoons or evenings to cool things off. My office and classroom were air-conditioned; but weekends were a problem: my top-floor flat was scorching at midday. After a few weekends of matinees, long lunches, and riding the air-cooled commuter train to Perth and back, I discovered an old limestone building with an almost monastic inner courtyard. There, in deep shade, I could listen to folk singers and poetry readings, could sip fruit drinks from the little snack shop and browse the indoor exhibits. I came to think of Fremantle's Art Centre and Museum as a place of refuge, refreshment, solace, not just from heat, but from the inevitable loneness of a stranger in a strange, though beautiful, land. The word "asylum" kept coming to my mind.

That word proved to be apt. When I got around to reading the Centre's brochure, I discovered that it was built in 1864 as the Fremantle Asylum for "Lunatics." Convict labor quarried the stone, native jarrah wood framed the rooms, and into them came men and women for whom there were no trains and electric fans, for whom the only way of coping with harsh and unforgiving terrain was to leave it, to let the mind slip its moorings even as the body remained. A new friend, Philippa Ryan, told me that a woman in her family tree had been committed there after the birth of her last child. Perhaps it was only postpartum depression, Philippa said, but according to family legend, the woman lived for years and years and never left the limestone walls.

That woman began to follow me. Her footsteps echoed as I moved from room to room in the Centre, as my heels rang on the old jarrah stairs. Though I flourished in Fremantle's unpolluted light, and became bold enough to make solo expeditions into the sunburnt plains beyond the escarpment, I always traveled with a sense of earlier travelers, of women who thrust themselves—or were thrust by their lives—into barely discovered countries of place, or position, or mind. Theirs were the lives I wanted to investigate. Theirs were the stories I wanted to tell.

Sonia Gernes
*Notre Dame, Indiana, 1997*

# The Indian School

Pipestone, Minnesota, 1930–31

*For my mother, Sophia Boerboom Gernes*

*These schools should be conducted upon lines best adapted to the development of character, and the formation of habits of industrial thrift and moral responsibility, which will prepare the pupil for the active responsibilities of citizenship.*

RULES FOR THE INDIAN SCHOOL SERVICE, p. 3

*Give the Indian a white man's chance. Educate him in the rudiments of our language, teach him to work . . . It will exterminate the Indian but develop a man.*

COMMISSIONER WILLIAM A. JONES, 1903

Home Economics Class, Indian Training School,
Pipestone, Minn.

## 1. Home Economics

I who said I would never teach
am learning now, white
girl caught in the stampede
of 1930, Pa's hatchery gone,
the gristmill faltering,
my fair-skinned love
wheeling amid the weaning calves,
the cows dried up, oats
still in shocks no one will buy,
a five-acre bog of potatoes.

The baby chicks,
his last nest-egg hope,
sucked beneath the floorboards—
seventeen in one night,
twenty-four the next,
a single rat wrapping its tail
round both our dreams.

And I here,
an endless plain away, white
in my apron and cap,
my baking powder, flour bins,
my recipes for shortbread,
dumplings, thrift. I,
for ninety dollars a month,
stumble into the brown distrust
of eyes that buy nothing,
give nothing away.

## 2. Civilization

Miss Perry says I should not decorate
with tepees, feathered hoops, the strange bent cross
girls doodle in the flour on their kneading boards.
(Miss Perry, nearly forty, is my cottage mate.)

Miss Perry says these kids don't need a nudge—
they go "back to the blanket" anyway
—to shacks and dogs and filthy pagan ways.
Miss Perry has been westward to Pine Ridge.

The rules come to us from Washington:
no blankets, no beads, no speaking in Sioux,
no hair worn long, no going home till June.
Miss Perry is sorry for the little ones.

We're here to show them the way, she says,
to make decent, Christian, tidy homes.
Miss Perry has a bible in her room.
I keep my rosary right beside the bed.

### 3. Postcards

Sept. 15, 1930

Dear Pa,

Yes, I'm glad you talked me into it,
and yes, the Ford is working fine.
But is it true the bank at Ghent has failed?
My summer's work gone up like air?
Write and tell me all you can.

Sept. 20, 1930

Dear Esther,

Well, kid, what's up with you?
Frank & Irma came down last week
to picnic in the quarry yard.
Frank kept making war whoops,
pretending he had a pipe to smoke.
He's such a card!

Sept. 24, 1930

Dearest A,

Do I look like this photo of Indian Joe?
The superintendent's wife
thought I was Sioux or Choctaw!
Can you imagine it—with my green eyes?

Think you'd like my hair in braids?
Think you'd like to kiss a squaw?

## 4. Radio

A Sunday of rain and no place to go,
the radio sighing: are you lonely tonight?

I think of your voice, your song,
that lane down the wooded ravines,
the flume where we kissed,
the river as broad as I dreamed.

No Yankton bands playing tonight,
none of that new, bubbly sound.
The road-map, spread out, goes
nowhere. Miss Perry has a cold,
is darning runs in her hose.

## 5. Hair

"They washed it in kerosene."
Mindy Lightfoot says,
and my skin crawls
the way it crawled
when I got chicken lice
cleaning out the coop.
"They didn't have to cut it too."

Mindy weeps above her darning hoop,
hair shorter than the chin-length bob
each girl is given Entrance Day.
"But look at mine," I say. "My dad
cut mine. Bobs are all the rage!"

I talk of freedom from all that weight
hanging down your neck, of prissy aunts,
of nuns who said it served me right
to freeze an ear for being vain.

"No," Mindy weeps, "No.
A woman's hair holds breeze
and breath and shining night—
a woman's hair is falling rain."

### 6. Influenza

Last night in the infirmary,
I watched the prairie thicken,
darkness viscous as the syrup
I dispensed for coughs. The nurse,
burning with a fever of her own,
left me only this instruction:
*keep them quieted down.*

Nine girls on first floor,
seven boys above, their breaths
a dozen tones of long-grass
weaving in a prairie wind.

How was I to recognize delirium—
a sudden terror moving through the beds,
Hector Esau jolting up,
crying out in Sioux?

"Speak English, Hector," I told him.
"It's a nightmare, a fever-dream.
Wake up!" But for all the good it did,
I might have been a milkweed fluff,
a peeping fledgling in the prairie's hum.

The current ran down both the rows.
"He sees somebody,"
Jimmy Tall Horse said,
"He sees in the window. This is bad."

"This is second floor," I said,
"there's nothing outside but night."

"Maybe it's his brother," Jimmy said.
"His brother died last year. Right here.
At night. Maybe they released his soul..."

"Maybe *who* released his soul?" I said,
but silence fell like a linen pall
across their eyes. "He couldn't go home,
he couldn't get real medicine..."
the smallest of them said,
and that was all.

I don't know who slept last night,
and who lay still, young rabbits
freezing to elude a hawk.
I prowled the rows of beds,
stalked the dark panes
for all I've heard:

witches and medicine-men,
raiders dead and alive,
sweat lodge and worshipped sun,
mumbo jumbo and all that's vile.

Morning came on schedule,
and none of my patients died.
But why was my report so brief:
        *one girl's fever broke,*
        *one boy had dreams.*

And did I imagine
those whispers through the night,
like a clear and distant bell:
        *Don't tell, Miss B.*
        *Don't tell. Don't tell.*

## 7. Diagnosis

I now know this:
Robert Esau had a cold,
(or asthma, or a touch of TB).
They sent him to the fields
where all the upper boys
shucked corn by hand—
a yield of golden missiles
tossed to farm-school wagon beds.

This was not right, he said.
No one thanked the corn,
no one made an offering.
He  refused to work,
got caned five strokes,
began to gasp and pant,
his body a feverish dawn.

How do you put out a fire
that's fed on belief?
He died young, that's all.
It happens frequently.

Now, the boys pick corn again,
drought-stunted ears in dusty rows.
But the dead do not dance
across the field. The dead
stay dead, the night unhaunted,
the windows blank.

The living
need to draw the line. I put mine
across my kneading board:
once bread is baked,
it does not rise again.
Nobody here
is Jesus.

## 8. Assembly: the Reverend Hubert Cole on Citizenship

Since this great nation, six years ago,
deemed it fitting to extend
citizenship to Indians and
(along with women) the right to vote,
it is incumbent on us all to note
what makes a good American:

> living upright Christian lives
> casting off our heathen ways,
> taking up work and honest labor,
> cleanliness in body, home and mind,
> being truthful and grateful and sober
> (drink being the curse of your people's lives).

Your teachers want the best for you:
farming, cooking, the civilizing arts.
Even the "great father" in Washington
tells me he has "an Indian heart . . ."

*Ahead of me, two football boys*
*elbow each other's ribs. One sputters*
*behind his hand, the other smirks.*
*I think I hear "Chief Wind-in-the-Gut."*

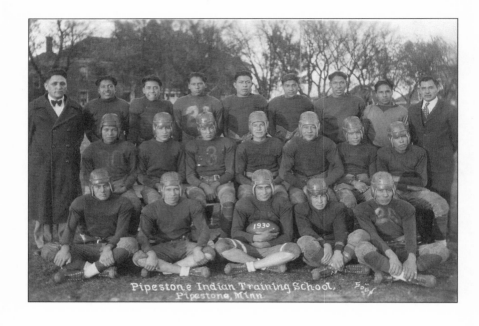

Pipestone Indian Training School,
Pipestone, Minn.

## 9. Scalp Day

The football team is fully garbed
in leather helmets, shoulder pads,
a glint of pride
breaking their defensive line
of routine sullenness.

My girls have made their shirts,
sewn numbers by which we score
acceptance of our ways.
Neat seams hold, I tell them; a stitch
in time could save nine yards
raveling out on the playing field.

*Homecoming,* we would have called it
in any other school—this pitting
of braves with braves
from Flandreau's institute—
but this is not home,
my girls tell me,
this is where you are taken
to change into someone else.

Nobody comes here, Mindy Lightfoot says.
Nobody simply *comes.*

## 10. Pipestone

Before they could approach
the quarry ledge,
they smoked kinnikinic—
tobacco, red willow bark,
a seasoning of prairie herbs.
They bathed in Winniwissa's stream,
left women in the camp, paused
at Wa-root-ka's sacred rocks,
to leave their sacrifice.

If, at daybreak, a totem appeared
scratched somewhere in the stone,
they were worthy to point
heavenward the lighted pipe,
point all four corners of the universe,
point downward to earth,
begging permission
to break her skin,
to find in her veins
this sacred stone.

Indian Joe in his quarry hut
told me this. He carves
paperweights, arrowheads,
the little pipe I'm sending you.

*Pipestone is part of our flesh,*
he said, *red men a part of this stone.*

*Then, why do you sell it?* I said,
looking off toward the quarry shelf.
*This is a place of peace,* he said,
*war clubs are buried, angers gone.*

*The seventh direction is self,*
he said. *When you white men pray,*
*does it come from breath—*
*does it come from bone?*

## 11. The Visit

Love,
all day the wind has blown
from west to east,
pushing you away from me,
pushing you home
in your old Model T,
past fields too dry
to sustain a house, a home—
lovers intent on a family.

My girls are glad
your hair is dark,
your face clean-shaved,
your ears delighted by
the music of their calendar:

> Moon of Strawberries
> Moon of Fattening
> Moon of Big Winds
> Moon of Cherries Blackening...

This is the moon
of the 2-cent stamp, of potatoes
16 cents a hundredweight,
of a heart sent to you
in cheap government ink,
a moon of longing,
a moon of constraint.

Love,
you are my one constant star,
but we've pledged ourselves
under a Depression moon,
that miserly changling
with his teasing game.
*"I'm full, I'm fuller,"* he taunts,

but here, now, on Indian land,
I am without you,
and already, already,
he's starting to wane.

## 12. Story Hour

Last night, late lightning hit—
thunder in a month of early snow.
Seven girls and I were setting up
for breakfast; seven girls who made
a dark aura round a lantern flame
when the generator failed to go.

Nothing to be scared of, I said,
forgetting they were used to night,
to candles, kerosene, oil lamps
from days of rendered buffalo fat.

Who knows a story, I said,
of lightning or thunder,
or trouble from the sky?

The darkness stirred with giggling.

> *Sometimes,*
> said Nellie Bird in her softest tone,
> *a giant turtle lowers its tail*
> *through all the layers of Father Sky.*
> *Sometimes that tail smacks Mother Earth,*
> *and white people call it "tornado."*

> *In the long ago* (another voice)
> *before we had to leave our land,*
> *heaven was different from now.*
> *A snowstorm of stars*
> *raced through the sky,*
> *and all the other stars*
> *danced and turned in their places.*

*In my grandma's time* (Edna Good Bear)
*thunder was an angry god,*
*and people had to dance—*
*the men in strange costumes,*
*the women in nothing*
*but eagle plumes and air.*

*At the end of the dance,*
said Delphine LaMere,
*they would pluck pieces of meat*
*from kettles boiling over a pit.*
*The dancers would plunge right in*
*and no one's hands were hurt*...

"You shouldn't tell that!" Mindy Lightfoot said
and stood. "Thunder dreamers are not talked about."

The darkness around me now was mute.
"Is there a legend about releasing souls?"
I said, but a stab of lightning split the room,
and then the thunder hit so hard
even the eye of our lantern flame
blinked and shuddered and shut.

## 13. Frog

When it was my turn,
I told them this:

Hay mowing time on my father's farm,
the noons liquid and pungent
as the buttermilk my brother and I
left cooling in the creek.

Resting time, and we hitched
the horses to the fence,
followed an eerie squeal
to a frog, its body motionless,
its terror shrill
before the swaying pendulum
of a bull snake's head.

We too were hypnotized.
The snake circled, a hoop of death,
swallowed one hind leg
and then the next, the jaw
opening like a vise.
I, unhinged as well,
could not move until
the bulging eyes went down.

My brother killed it.
Beat the head with a rock
and slit that scaly belly
with his pocket knife.

This is the amazing part:
the frog jumped free. Alive

and energetic—Jonah
from the whale—it beat the spell,
the serpent's eyes, the wakeful
force that can swallow you whole.

*This is the part I did not tell:*
*when I rise each day*
*with my recipes*
*am I the knife or the snake?*

## 14. Spheres

I was my father's oldest,
his right-hand girl, his "hired man,"
preening as we harnessed the Clydesdales,
the Belgian roans, a double team
for the four-gang plow I alone
was old enough to manage.

          That spring,
when his peacocks were molting,
when I tucked an iridescent eye
into each brass bridle ring
and plowed the corner turns
precise as quilted squares,
I measured time by the gold
of his pocket watch, dreaming
as it slipped its chain, planted itself
somewhere in the back quarter section.

I knew that time does not reverse itself,
that pride precedes an object's fall,
that the losses we sow
we must also reap, but my father
who knew nothing of circles
in Indian lore, said only,
"Maybe it will sprout,"
reached, and ruffled my hair.

       *Imagine a gold seed ticking.*
       *Imagine slender stalks like minute hands.*
       *Imagine each blossom giving us back*
       *some piece of the past that we've used up.*

*Imagine life*
*as a circle of days, a ring of years,*
*a bright and burnished hoop*
*that brings us back*
*to each of our beginnings.*

## 15. Flight

A new crisis in the night:
seven girls descending
a plait of sheets, a white
license to freedom, to home,
to boys waiting
in the shadowed stalls
of the dairy barn.

Six girls down safely,
the seventh easing out—
then a linen rip, a shriek,
a sound like melons
dropping from a truck,
slim shadows dispersing,
the house mother running
across the ruptured dark.

The seventh girl
may never be right.
The doctor does not know
if the silence in her eyes
is forgetfulness or dream:
herself on a pale horse riding,
her long, long hair a stream
of cloud—or herself scenting
the darkness of a stall,
a boy's stone face relenting,
his hand moving downward,
her lips forming *ooh*,
the soft-eyed Jerseys
who give us cream
watching all
and whatever they do.

## 16. Morning Report

Two girls were out all night,
Miss Perry says, three boys
still missing, two expelled,
shipped off to their tribe's "Res"
or one of the Reformatory Schools.

It happens all the time, she says,
no gratitude for what we've done:
the chances to improve themselves,
good meals and clothes and tools.

We always get them back, she says:
Delphine LaMere, cracked head and all,
Edna Goodbear, the Lightfoot girl . . .
Still missing are the oldest Platt,
that Esau boy who believes in spooks,
some other fool.

"But won't they freeze?" I say.
"It's late November now.
The fields are slick with rime."

"They know how to burrow in,"
she says, "Haven't you noticed?
Like groundhogs or gophers,
like frogs in the mud of a pool."

### 17. Virtue

Why this small itch
of envy in the dark,
this urge to step out on air,
fibers of flax my only safety,
night my only coat?

I have never raced toward dawn
in a lover's arms. Each night I wear
a winding sheet of purity,
a daytime dress of duty and belief.
No leaping a bareback horse,
hands thrust into the mane,
no moon for a rudder,
no steering by the breeze.

## 18. Midnight

My first taste of midnight
was the time I helped with lambing,
the year that I was twelve.
I did not know then
that any female opening
was made so wide, so wet,
so full of slime and slippery coatings,
slick as stock-tank algae
afloat in summer shade.

When it was over,
I went to stand at the barn's half-door,
the moon a silver sickle,
the stars just out of reach.
Pa came to stand beside me
but we did not speak.

The prairie was a band of blackness,
the wind a lowing sound. I knew,
for him, that *longing* meant the old,
the other country; for me, new space
to enter in. But both of us
were standing at love's margin,
at the vast ache of a treeless plain
where nothing calls and nothing moves
except the lower layers of your skin.

## 19. Bounty

Mindy will not speak to me.
She sulks behind her sewing tasks—
mending a three-corner tear,
matching plaids. She cleans
the cottage after school (one penalty
for having flown), sweeps and dusts
at tortoise speed—a calibrated scorn.

"Why did you do it?" I repeat.
"Weren't you afraid you'd freeze?
And where did Hector Esau go?"
But Mindy turns her back to me,
throws sweeping compound down.

"Is Hector with his folks?" I say.
"Hiding in some farmer's shed?
And how did *you* get caught?"
She makes of the compound a tepee form.
"Like animals," she finally says.

"They give the farmer money
to bring us back—like they do for pests
that dig up crops or kill the sheep."
She drops the broom, the dusting pan,
heads for the door. "Mindy, come back,"
I call, but my brother's image comes instead,
baiting the iron of his gopher traps,
salting the long-clawed front feet
to confirm his catch, a penny a pair,
his stinking tobacco cans
stuck in the rafters of the shed.

"Come back," I call again,
but the distance now is plain: I love a farmer,
and farmers need fields, need homes.
How could we give this prairie back again
to those who merely burrow,
merely roam?

## 20. Sleds

A strange Christmas—
walking under starlight
to Midnight mass,
the student heads black
before me, the earth
an indigo white.

Four hundred sacks
of candy and nuts ,
four hundred children
in the topsy-turved world
of staff who wait tables,
of Indians who sit
and giggle when served.

Movies and basketball
to fill the time, to fend
off tears of home, of fry-bread
and sledding hills, of grandpas
who once made sleds of buffalo-rib,
lacing together the smaller ends.

Love, on this flat horizon,
I wear each night the robe you sent.
I dream of hills, of woodlands,
of curling myself inside your arms
as those grandfathers curled
in their buffalo sleds,
a beating heart in a double cage
of ribs, a heart secure and safe
whatever the weather portends.

## 21. Assembly: the Man from Antarctica

*As the sun went down for the last time, the*
*darkness closed in and the aurora jerked*
*into fantastic patterns across the sky.*

ADMIRAL RICHARD BYRD

Imagine months of night,
he says; imagine cold so brisk
it would break your whiskers off.
Imagine life as moles
tunnelling from hut to hut
beneath a sky of snow.

Some men had visions, he says:
sun sparking the snow like flint,
frozen lakes aflame, infernos
of ice, light igniting
at the back of the eye.

Some ate blubber, he says;
some ate dog. Some ate nothing,
and staggered whirling
through dervishes of snow.

Why do men do this?
Why fast, why freeze,
why sweat as the Dakota do
in a stinking lodge?
Is there another world this side of death
where the "great mysterious"
truly can be known?

*Imagine a compass pointing*
*straight up to the sky.*
*Imagine a day of shadowless sun.*

*Imagine a crevasse so deep*
*that as you fall*
*rainbows shatter beside you.*

*Imagine a magnet pulling.*
*Imagine your own true north.*

## 22. Special Delivery

*It shall be the duty of superintendents. . .to*
*receive and control all mail matter addressed to*
*pupils. . .and to withold the same from delivery*
*where, in their opinion, it contains unmailable or*
*otherwise improper communication or articles.*
RULES FOR THE INDIAN SCHOOL SERVICE, p. 10.

A package arrived today
(by eagle? by sled?)
a student-issue shirt,
a handerchief stamped
*H. Esau/Gov't Property,*
a note that said: "This
for the braids you cut off
and sent to Ma at home."

No postmark, no stamps,
no witness, of course,
no one who saw anyone
take anything at all
down to the principal's office.

Miss Perry says
they were always sly,
those Esau boys,
their father dead,
their mother with eight
in a tar-paper shack,
the tribal council nodding
when the Agent said
"Pipestone,"
agreeing it was best.

The boys stayed through summer
almost every year,
hung around the carvers
at the quarry pits,
hauled flesh-colored stones
to the canker of tents
emerging like locusts
from the grass each June,
listened to the stories.

That's where the problem began,
Miss Perry says:
they listened to the stories.

## 23. Quarry

In a stuccoed corridor the photo hangs:
fourteen Indians, nine white chiefs
smoking a pipe on the quarry ledge.
Standing Bull (age 80) sits;
Myron Cohen, U. S. Court of Claims,
waits his turn with hand outstretched,
and Jennings Wise, attorney-at-law,
reads "The Peace Pipe," from *Hiawatha.*

No evidence
of food or drink; no lunch
on this soft stone,
this heart of earth,
the color of blood,
the color of the sacred.
The pie has already been cut
in Cohen's court,
a dollar value set
on the Pipestone reservation.

I think of that other *quarry:*
the hunted, the soon-to-be
consumed: the hawk
and the mouse, the deerslayer
silent on the forest leaves,
Major H. H. Rice
on his way home to Washington,
stalking the train's swift halls
in his new moccasins, waiting
for the deal to take effect, waiting
for darkness to fall.

## 24.  February 14:

What kind of valentine is this—
Uncle Jake at my cottage door,
the cap in his hands
a thick and blackened tongue?

"Your Pa," he says,
as if words were scarce
as everything else.
"Brain fever. Four days now.
The priest has come."

How can I imagine this—
my father's brain red as sun
above a seared horizon,
red as blood
from a chicken's severed neck?

*Encephalitis*, a manly, scientific word;
*coma*, as soft as female sleep.
My father wedding these two
inside his skull, inside a lining
so brilliant I must close my eyes
against the burning
of this February snow.

We are travelling now.
The black box of my uncle's Ford
turns north, careens across
a plane so white the roads
are mere intrusions, soft dents
in a future that will be hard,
hard.

## 25. Storm

All day I have walked a shadowless plane,
the sky white, the sun a lamp suspended
behind a scrim of linen sheets.

My feet are numb, my bones
keep asking: where is my father now?
In some green pasture of harp and dove?
Or here, here at the quarry's cusp,
knowing he exists, but differently—
his soul an arctic freedom
of endless white, endless plain,
endless, endless light?

## 26. Release

Hector, when his brother died,
slashed both his arms, sliced
in half his blankets and his sheets,
gave away the pipestone bits
he'd been allowed to keep.

No suicide attempt, Miss Perry says;
some old and pagan custom
about the way to grieve.

"Did they keep his soul"?
I ask, "—the brother's soul?"

"Oh, that," Miss Perry laughs.
"The government—the B.I.A.—
banned that nonsense
forty years ago—ordered
the Sioux on a certain day
to release all souls they kept."

But who could check
if they did or not?—and where
do freed souls go?

Did they swirl like genies
from the tepee's center hole?
Did they rush long and low
scaring the prairie grass
like bobcats gaining speed?

To keep a soul within a house
would be to let all earthly things

give way. To fast and weep,
and sleep upon a bed
of sacred sage, the mind
a sheet stretched out
to capture any dreams.

To keep a soul
would be a lover's act,
a wild flower pressed
at dawn each day, a lock
of hair in a well-worn book,
a horizon so clean and bare
you'd sense a presence there at once,
no matter how empty it seemed.

## 27. Air Waves

Ever since the diphtheria shot,
I've been feeling strange, unsettled.
Other "medicines" seem to be at work.
My honey writes: "Dream a little dream of me,"
but I sleep badly. I lie and wonder
what face looms behind the window shade,
what shadow on the wall
has traveled to get here,
has slipped inside
as easily as sound.

If a voice from Sioux Falls
can ride through the night
on nothing but air,
what of souls, of shapes, of shadows?

My thoughts clog
like damp flax binding up the reaper.
Father, are you here now?

## 28. Washun Niya: Wind Cave, the Black Hills

This is what Mindy says
about the place of grief:

Hunting with friends, Taopi Gli,
the noble warrior, son of chiefs,
wandered into shadow,
was seen talking to a canyon maid—
her dress of doeskin, her headress of light,
hair like a wet otter's sheen.
Then he vanished—
like ghosts, like dreams,
like the woman Persephone
in our sophomore Latin text.

But this is the difference:
he never came back.
No pomegranate, no mix
of springtime flowers
or summer of plumping fruit.
After they'd mourned him,
and shorn their hair, and risked
their lives on a vision quest,
they had only the flute of breath,
the song of sighing, the still vacuum
that cavorts with life.

But Washun Niya,
*the hole that breathes cool air,*
whispered forth deer for them,
elk, the huge-headed buffalo.

Who whispers for us?
—Ma with all those children
still home to raise alone—
my Love in his potato fields
forking our future tine by tine?

No breeze of plenty
thaws out this land. The breath
clearing frost from the window pane
is mine, is mine.

## 29. Postage

Mindy today in the sewing room,
her darning done, her scraps
swept up, sews contraband beads
on a palm-sized pouch
made from bits of mattress ticking.

"When you go to town," she says,
"do you get mushy notes
from your honey-boy?
Do you buy stamps? Seal
your letters with a kiss?
Would you like to have
this pretty little bundle?"

"What's this about?" I say,
but she drops her head,
turns coy: "In the long-ago,
warriors sent notched sticks,
codes of love, to maidens
off in another village."

"Are you writing to Hector?"
I say. "Did *you* smuggle in
that hankie and shirt?"

She knots the thread
of an unfinished rose;
her eyes avert. "Now
Hector's sixteen," she says.
"He doesn't have to come back.
See," she says, "you could use
this pouch for stamps and notes.

It could be a place to keep them.
You could bring it back next week
for me to finish hemming."

"You know the rules," I say.
"All mail goes through the matron,
and I wouldn't let Miss Perry
catch you with those beads."

Though what's the harm,
I think, in a single stamp?
My own future might as well
be notched on willow wands;
any one of these winds
could take it away.

## 30. Arbor Day

*Pupils should be instructed as to the value
of forest and fruit tree culture . . .*
RULES FOR THE INDIAN SCHOOL SERVICE, p. 27

We are planting Russian olive trees,
box elder, ash, a windbreak of elm
where the wind, unbroken, used to hum
its low and constant song.
We are trying to teach them
stewardship.

Every farm here has its grove—
its homestead stake
of living wood, its claim
to hold the earth, to own
this land, to plow down
what the winds have borne
and raise up fields of grain.

The missing things
are little things, Miss Perry says,
and not much use. Indian Joe
can recite them for you:

> chokecherry, bergamot,
> ground plum, prairie rose,
> tiger lily, buffalo berry,
> lance-leaved sage,
> anemone . . .

For fifty cents
he'll carve an arrowhead,
a totem, a rough-edged petroglyph
of something you have never seen:

> whooping crane, burrowing owl,
> prairie chicken, upland plover,
> longspur, and his favorite,
> which says its name in dreams:

> *will, will, willet* . . .
> *will, will, willet* . . .

## 31. Dust Storm

We are all outlaws now.
Kerchiefs over the nose and chin,
we scuttle from dorm to workshop,
from cottage to laundry room,
our bodies bent against an enemy
insidious as sin.

Past the dairy barn, topsoil sifts
against the fenceposts, drifting
like snow, like mourning crepe
sagged across a bier.

Will even the land leave us?

O my Love—there on your farm
above the Mississippi—
set the fenceposts deeply,
plow in contours around the hills,
keep, preserve, retain
the hope that we can be together,
that our feet in the soil
will bring not dust but rain.

## 32. Calumet

White Buffalo Woman,
she who walked out of mystery
into a Lakota camp,
had a red pipe in her bundle.

> *The bowl of red stone is Mother Earth*
> *The carved calf is the four-legs who live upon her*
> *The stem is the wood of all that grows*
> *The feathers of all that soars*
> *Every dawn is a holy event*
> *Every step on our Mother a prayer*
> *With Wakan Tanka I am walking...*

What is that, I ask Mindy—*Wakan Tanka?*

The Great Mysterious, she says,
breath you can see, breath that creates,
life breath of the universe.
Do you believe me?

I believe in the Catholic God, I say:
Father, Son and Holy Ghost.

I hear myself say it:  *Holy*

*Ghost.*

### 33. Vision Quest:

I don't know how to do this.
I've fasted through supper,
put a tiny tear in my best chemise,
lit a candle (illegal here),
prayed the rosary twice.

The Sioux seek answers
on a mountaintop, bring
tobacco and feathers
as an offering—
eagle or crow or hawk.

It makes good sense; winged
creatures are close to heaven,
but I have far too much
to do with earth:
> Should I teach
> and give my mother money?
> Try to take my father's place?
> Marry for love, but share
> a house with in-law strangers?
> Stay but risk a transfer
> to Oklahoma, to bare
> tedium at Rosebud
> or Pine Ridge?

I want to dream of cows—
pink, swaying udders,
soft, female breath.
I want to see my Love
move in that fertile moisture,

down rows and rows of stanchions
with frothy pails of milk.

I am willing to suffer hunger
for a body that is fecund.
I am willing to give up certainty
for a vision of my own.

### 34. Blaze

What is not dust
is smoke. This evening
when the sky due south
lit like a sunrise in June,
I bypassed the matron,
filled the Ford
with ninth-grade girls,
drove them to watch
wheat turn to flame—
elevators burning
on the highway to Trotsky.

Indian fires, my students say,
clean the land, help catch
small game, let everything
start fresh. White fires
—wheat or not—
are always the same: first,
you gather too much in one spot;
then, when earth can't hold
the weight, sky sends a spark
to suck up tons
of heavy smoke.

"Not true," I laugh,
"smoke doesn't weigh,"
but they stick to their guns:
"Try weighing a log,"
the Good Bear twins say;
"try weighing the ash
when the log is gone."

I know science better than that,
but something weighs here
that I want to lose. Already
I've lightened the rule book,
filled Mindy's little stamp-pouch
and let it do its work.

Home again, girls spill
from the Ford, run
toward the dorm. "Mindy!"
I call, before she runs too far.
"Look, there's a letter I forgot—
there, in the glove box of my car."

## 35. Dream:

I am pushing through brambles
and the slope is steep, steep
sliding down through bloodroot,
ladyslipper, frosted white stems
you call Indian pipe, and it's
the blackberry patch,
you tell me, we live in the tangle
of thorn and fruit, but I slip,
skid down the ravine
to the flume, the wooden chute,
black with tar, that will keep,
you say, our fields from eroding,
and I reach out a hand,
call my father's name, but it's you,
you who hold me, who say
I must turn fear to smoke, pack
my bags, an immigrant
bride with a dowry of dust,
rich in the act of letting go,

and when I wake
the sun is skimming mist
from the clover fields, and
it seems that I have always known
precisely this:

Father, I will marry him.
Father, I release your soul.

## 36. Totems

I take with me, from Indian Joe,
a horseshoe carved for "white man's luck,"
from Mindy, a little pipestone book,
a feather I suspect that Hector sent,
a rug Miss Perry hooked.

My sacred hoop is now a wedding band,
and of the four directions, I choose east,
but I will this prairie to stay in my bones—
this quarry, where every stone speaks peace.

# The Mutes of Sleepy Eye

Sleepy Eye, Minnesota, 1968

*this time, for Carole Glickfeld*

## 1. CLARA

The train,
when we had one,
would come through here
like an Angus bull
looking for a herd in heat.
Snorting, pawing
at the station, at
the neon eye
of the old hotel's
Bar & Lunch.

They used to put me on it,
tagged like a turkey,
my brother's boots
and my stockings hitched up,
back and forth
to the Faribault schools
for the feeble-minded,
deaf and dumb. Mama
printed DEAF
in letters big as wooden blocks;
I'd stumble on the tears,
the hard-edged seats
that scratched my thighs
where the stockings left me short.

Eyes on the train
scratched at the paper
pinned to my coat: "DEAF.
*Will be met at Owatonna*
*by Faribault staff."*

She might as well
have printed DUMB.
My face, working to say
I feared this bull,
looked feeble enough
—feared this headlong race
through fences and over ties
that should have kept me home.

They taught me the sign: *deaf:*
*ear closed.*
But eyes on the train
took the paper from my coat
and closed it around my mind.
DUMB. The same as STUPID.
Hopeless, bricked in
by rows of silent cots,
the FEEBLE MINDED
only a road away. A dumb
child from Sleepy Eye.

That spring, I learned to sign.
My hands woke.
My fingers flew away.

## 2. CLARA

Sleepy Eye is an Indian's name,
these Germans tell me,
though somebody, sometime
decoded it. Not Waseca,
Mankato, Minnehaha.
Not laughing water, not Winona,
the Indian maid who leaped
to an old river's arms
rather than take
a warrior unloved. Not
Minnetonka, Minneota,
not Owatonna or Wanamingo,
but Sleepy Eye.
A name like a joke.
A name I knew they called
on that train coming home
with scratchy stockings
from the Faribault school
for deaf and dumb.

The Conductor would stride
through the car, mouth open
for the familiar round:
*Mankato, New Ulm, Sleepy Eye.*
I would feel him come as horses feel
the air before the storm.
His face would bawl the names,
and then he'd bend, mouthing
like a circus clown
the words pinned to my coat.
The name had whiskey breath,
hairy arms to lift my suitcase down.

*Sleepy Eye. Sleepy Eye.*
That would wake them—
the bored travelers, unlabeled,
unsought. "Is that for real?"
their lips would say. "Is that a town?"
Is that a joke somebody played
on three-thousand four-hundred and sixty-
one poor, dumb, German, settler souls?

Not New Ulm. Not Ghent. Not New Prague.
Not a place to take old roots like potatoes
and stick them in the virgin ground.
Not St. Peter or St. Cloud or Harmony.
Not even Blue Earth.
Sleepy Eye.

Sleepy Eye,
Chief of the Sisseton Sioux.

Is that why we got this land?
Did they hand down his fate with his name?
Did some early warrior chief forget
that victory never sleeps?
Did some boy-child coming
from the blood-lined sack
into the tepee's leather womb
look first on a crone
too tired to midwife in the dawn?
Did he look on an aged and lazy dog?

Or was it a woman—
young limbs like sturdy birch
when the moon reveals
fingers of wind
teasing through the leaves?
Were her eyes the cause
of a careless watch,
a deep and endless sleep?

Or did they think that one Great Eye
like the eye of a cat
bored with her grown young
watched all the silent deeds of men;
one Great Eye
still and barely
open.

## 3. CLARA

At Faribault, I learned to read.
Words, like alphabet blocks
dumped on the page, were stacked,
teetered, began to have vibrations.
They moved in my head
like the winter a deep purr moved
in a telephone pole. *So this is sound,*
I thought: a cheek shivered
against trembling wood, a shudder
that wants to get out. Our hound
would strain against the collar,
my hands feeling what escaped
("howl" they called it), like the quake
of the train before it charged.

*So this is talk,* I thought
when words on the page began to bob
like lips that mimed the life I wanted.

You cannot live in books.

The summer I came home
half-trained to teach the deaf,
Wilbur signed: You marry me?
I was twenty-one. His hands
were roots, a rich, firm pulp

73

to probe the dark. His words
were grain bins, seeds, a rump
of beef. He signed away
my shyness. Our children
lit in his arms like butterflies,
their voices a flicker of breeze
he could not believe. I know
two languages. This one runs
like children on the page;
the other turns whole mounds
of air. The Kaufmann girl
kicks up words like a colt on sod,
her brother's hands useless as a tail.
My fingers are quiet now.

When Wilbur lived,
no animals burrowed quite so deep.

## 4. CLARA

They never sent the Kaufmann boy to school.

He saw the train
charge past the old home farm
where he'd pull at blackcaps
on the section fence, his eyes
like moons in a bramble patch.

They wired him instead. A plug
in his ear, and two stiff tendrils
twining down his neck. He's
the one looks feeble-minded,
watching their mouths
with his mouth open. Aunt Bert
wrote on a scratch pad once:
"Sounds like a screech owl. Can't
understand a word he says."

When the girl came, Elise,
a package delivered ten years late,
she got sent to Faribault. The brother
watched like a tall, daft horse
when her hands began to speak.

More colt than anything,
she gallops now to basketball
and movie shows. Her hands
move like startled birds,
like sharp-fingered clouds
across the space
where his eyes are caught
still dark,
still mooning.

## 5. DELBERT

My sister
has round tits now
cow eyes
round ass that swings
like udders full of milk.
She walks too close
to gutters. Somebody
playing in the barn.

## 6. ELISE

Why they wired him to his belly-button
I'll never know. Those batteries,
like some bowl of sound,
are supposed to feed
what isn't in his head.
I've seen people cringe
when he tries to talk.
Better to be dumb
than stupid. Besides,
how can he hear?
He sees too much.

## 7. CLARA

So there are three of us
since Wilbur died. Two Kaufmanns
pacing off their ties
to a farm by the railroad tracks;
me, stitching together
a life in town. I own

this house, this space
beneath the cottonwoods
where my daughter
Carol's children whoop
and turn into Indians,
where their fat hands skin
bullheads from the lake.

Todd is my resident foreigner.
He knows to sign, learned it
as fingers learn to turn a tap,
to lift the lid on the cookie jar.
Now, his hands are stuck
in the pockets of his jeans.

Seventeen is a foreign land.

## 8. DELBERT

Thirteen.
Pa hit with his belt
not for peeing
for shooting sticky seed
at targets on the barn.

What else
was it good for?

Older is not much better.
Still nothing
but hardness in the dark.
Nothing to aim for. No names
I can pronounce.

## 9. ELISE

A caterpillar
crawled in my dream last night,
eyeless, and big as my thumb.
It crawled over my belly, my breasts
wanting a place to hibernate,
to spin small threads of light,
to find a way of nudging in.

The usual sickness woke me.
It was still dark, but something new:
butterfly wings
awake and beating
in the blackness of my gut.

This is what
that furry worm has left.

## 10. FATHER TRACY

The mass is all in English now;
we get our hymns from the protestants;
confession is face-to-face, and
mystery drove off in a pick-up truck.

If St. Paul were here, no doubt
he'd give out feed-store caps.
Instead of *Doughboy* or *Super-gro*
the visor would say: *Jesus saves.*

## 11. CLARA

In the Catholic church
they have some kind of holy water.
Blue-skirted angels
balancing scallop shells
hold it on their heads.

This town is like that
only upside down:
first, a shallow basin of streets,
then grain elevators
holding the sky off the ground.

## 12. FATHER TRACY

Christ! What next?
My assistant leaves,
they expect me to help
at the migrant camps,
explain to these farmers
what it means to tithe,
and set up a religion class
because the blasted nuns
are trooping off to ghetto work
*en masse*. And then—
some seventeen-year-old
deaf & dumb kid
gets herself knocked up!

One of the nuns
can handle it.
Maybe writing on a chalkboard
will be more relevant
when that and a bastard
are both in your lap.

## 13. SISTER JOAN OF ARC

So he says:
*I'll give you* social work
if you're so sure
that's where it's at.
But how do you intend to tell her
you have to *hear* to hear
it crying in the dark?

I think she hears what matters.
She walks as though her body lifts
to music from the womb, to all
the melodies that women rise to: hands
playing down the scale to secret flesh,
a small drum beating, the horn
of a mouth on a well-tuned breast.

Bless me Father, for I am normal.

She and I were sisters before,
wearing silence like a veil
around our longing. Now
a tiny tambourine
clicks against her cloister walls.
Some minstral's instrument
has gotten in. Bless

me, Father. If I told you
all women want to dance
to castanets, would any tune
get through?

## 14. FATHER TRACY

Words were made flesh
once, on a train across Bavaria,
by a gamekeeper's daughter
with eyes like a hare's
and a crown of braids like wheat
fields where you could roam forever.

I was twenty-five, in ski clothes,
a cap on my freshly tonsured head.
The seminary vanished down the track
like some ancient flag of Rome.

I never touched her.
Her voice touched everything:
goats, birds, the upland fields.
The train sang until dusk:
a litany of feathered words, of
mating calls, of small game
that rise nocturnally
feeding in the pouch of night.

She was the earth. She
was the name a city child has
for meadows, that hunger has
for milk. For the first time
words were palpable—a rabbit
nestling in the palm, a field mouse,
a rare and quivering thrush.

Minnesota had a new diocese
when I returned: a sea of farm lands,
hamlets, the hearty bosom

of garden crops. I thought
God and the gamekeeper's daughter
had rolled into one. I left
Dante and Aquinas, philosophy,
the cities I had planned to page
like venerated books. I would be
the shepherd, the sower of seed,
the keeper of the living Word.
I would go.

That was 1957. Year by year,
the highway westward flattened,
the land was milked by great machines,
small game fled from snowmobiles,
sameness ran through fingers
as fast as wheat. Now I have names
for nothing. My sermons
have gotten shorter; prayers
roll off the mimeograph. The local paper
is the closest thing to soil
I care to dig at.

One pays a price for loving idols:
feathered words are bound to migrate.
Each spring, less and less return.

## 15. NETTIE

I said to Jake:

in Clara's day
the dummies didn't even sign
in public. Humped over like little snails,
they'd twitch their fingers quick
then draw them in like feelers.
Jake says:

Humped is the word, all right.

Don't talk dirt, I says.
Of course, they should have
a normal life, not stay in a shell.
I'm all for that. But now look
what's out and showing!

## 16. DELBERT

She didn't do it in town.

New lamps they put on streets
have eyes
long and mean
as tomcats.

All night
they never sleep.

## 17. JENKINS

It wouldn't surprise me none
if that brother done it himself.
They raised that boy
like a steer. It's long
past time he noticed
there's heifers in the lot.

Maybe he thought he'd trip
on that wire round his neck
if he jumped any fence
but one. I blame their old man.
He ought to know what's in heat
and, for God's sake, when!

## 18. DELBERT

Mr. Jenkins
feed store man
got eyes like owl
watching mouse.
No help this time.
I load ten sacks
Hog Concentrate;
owl-eyes watch.

But why throw in free
two packs
watermelon seed?

## 19. SISTER JOAN OF ARC

One night in the novitiate
I sneaked past halls of nuns
exhaling goodness through their veils
of sleep, out past the orchard hill
where the old red barn
lay beached and bleaching
by the covered swing.

Pulling knees to breasts
for warmth, I tuned myself
to what floated from below:
uneven traffic, a restless dog,
voices from the open cars
that crooned like snatches
from a radio: *What I'd give
for a little lovin'*...

I thought of how
our novice veils
sailed the apple trees;
days moved through silence
like dreamers in a wind;
how nothing touched.

Low laughter from cars
parked beneath the hill.
The moon moved closer—
a melon slice, cool and lush.

Tomorrow, the novices
would stand in line
to confess their sins;
would heap desires
in a laundry cart,
scrub down coifs and collars
till knuckles bled,
walk correct and closed
as safety pins.

I made a pact with God:

I would stay and give
my silence for such slivers of joy
as that April moon, my Aprils
for a slice of peace, however thin.
I would keep the rule
book in my deepest pocket,
the psalms within my head.
To sleep securely in a holy love,
washed and safe and pleasing,
I would walk into the cloistered dark.

The moon went down
before the Matins bell
and I came in.

## 20. CLARA

What if it was my son?

## 21. CLARA

Todd
(I'd like to say),
I forgive the hands
that refuse to touch
a language for the dumb,
the sounds you forge,
linking like a ladder
you can't wait to climb
from a mother's silent house.

I forgive the hands
welded to the pockets
of those worn-out jeans.

Todd
(I'd like to say),
are you sure?
Are you sure
you've been careful to keep
everything else tucked in?

## 22. SISTER JOAN OF ARC

It's the sounds that tempt me.
The eye has a cover.
The ear is a tunnel
into a slippery dark.

## 23. TODD

My mother knows about the grass.

She left the Mankato paper
open to this:
"U Students Nabbed in Drug Bust."

Out here, they string you up
for possession of an ounce.
Wouldn't be the first time
some poor bastard
got the short end of a rope.
They did it to the Sioux.

The Great Uprising of 1862!
Good as a western on the late, late show:
flashing tomahawks and bleeding maids.
And after the chase scenes,
thirty-eight buggers swung at once
while all Mankato cheered and waved.

"Like it or lump it,"
Aunt Nettie says,
"People get what they deserve."


Sure. Why not? It's a warning.
They teach it in sixth grade:
we're the folks who engineered
the biggest fucking execution
this country ever staged.

## 24. CLARA

A few years after the railroad came,
they changed the town's name
to Loreno.

It sounded like
an Italian opera star
charged by the bull
and running.

Two years later in '81
they changed it back.
Nobody wanted
to be that awake.

## 25. ELISE

The social worker
carries a little pad
so she can talk of holes;
gives me government pamphlets
about the body's openings—
what should and should not
go in. We had signs
for that in school: Put
a banana in your ear, a finger
up your nose, and keep
your knees shut tight. These
are different ones: buy jelly by the jar,
insert a rubber disk, stick seaweed
up the inner hole, and pump
a fetus out.

I don't get it.

It's like a story in school:
a deaf woman helped a blind man
to cross the street; could see
her silence irked him.

She signed the problem: deaf,
dumb, *opening closed*,
her finger on his ear, his lips.
That's when he began
to beat her with his cane.

So what's the moral?
Never put your finger
in a blind man's ear?

## 26. FATHER TRACY

Why does that girl bother me?
It's as though I think
the silent can't conceive.

She has a secret language.
When she doesn't know I'm watching,
the hands talk to themselves, gulp
small words the way a heron gulps fish.

But when I talk to her directly,
the herons in her hands become extinct;
she cradles her stomach, eyes tensed like a rabbit,
the small hands ready to sprint.

Do I chase the language from her?
Does she never blink?

## 27. ELISE

The sun fathered it.

The hearing say the wind makes noise—
howls like a hound's stretched throat.
Maybe so. But they think
the sun is silent.

I have heard it clink
off water in the creek
at the bend beyond the cottonwoods,
purr as it curls round and round
a long-grass nest, sniff
the clover growing in that
abandoned tractor seat.

The sun came in one afternoon
barefoot on the oaken floor, put
a warm hand on the small of my back,
touched, lightly as a breath,
my arm, the downy hair.
He leaned back first
on the leather couch,
pulled me gently down.

How could I see
what was happening?
There was sun in my eyes,
and when I closed them,
so much warmth I could drown.

## 28. FATHER TRACY

That deaf girl has
gotten in my dreams:

We were stalking pheasants
through fields of stripped
November corn. Each time

I felled a bird, she stooped,
held it to her belly,
watched it quicken, stretch,

fly away without a sound.
The gun was noiseless
as an eye; I could not see

if we were stalking silence
or words or a pantomime
of wings. Just before I woke

she handed me a bleeding bird
and spoke distinctly:

*These birds do not sing.*

*The important thing*
*is that they fly.*
*They fly*

## 29. ELISE

When you have words
you do not dream
as much.

My mother died
when *warmth* was still
an aproned lap, *spring*
was birds and rhubarb sauce
*father* was hands, faint
silage smells; *summer*
the sweet chewing
on a timothy stalk.

I did not know
names could stop the dream
of that shining box,
the pillow sheen beneath her,
the lid snapping shut.

I dreamed of stove pipes
that would suck you in,
the round press
of the sausage machine,
of coal chutes
that could slide you down
faster than a load
of tumbling dark.

*Coffin* is a word
I can write, can sign,
but my mind plays tricks.
*Chute*, I think, *pipe*,
*an open mouth.*

*Grave,* I sign,
but I am seeing *tunnel*
earth's long, dry throat.
I am thinking:
*caves, tornado clouds,*
*a deep, deep well,*
*a bucket that falls*
*from the end of the rope.*

## 30. CLARA

Nettie says
for two hundred dollars
those city people
can vacuum it out,
but what about the roots?

Strawberry plants,
the red cores of summer,
put out runners to keep
their grip on earth.
Small things hold on.

So what will she say
if they ask her:
*I'd be much obliged?*
*Go to hell?*
*The priest forbids it?*

Would she ever think to say:
*around my farthest rib*
*a filament winds*
*in the sweet loam of the dark.*

## 31. SISTER JOAN OF ARC

I have learned three words in sign:

*Baby* is arms cradled on the breast,
*boy,* a cap that peaks for baseball
or years of haying in the sun;
*girl* is a bonnet strap, a tautness
that has always held her down.

I watched Elise finger-spell;
her name is all tight fists
except where an "i" peeks out,
a bold "I" thumbs its way
into or out of trouble.

My name is a closing off.
The "j" swings freely first,
the "o" invites entry;
but then the "a" clamps down
like a conscience,
the "n" stays tight
like a half-forgotten vow.

Perhaps that's the secret:
break out of your name;
don't settle for an ending
where the thumb sneaks in and hides.

## 32. CLARA

The young nun who talks to Elise
is gone for a week
to a place called "retreat"
where no one talks—

but is that so different?
For years they've walked in twos
counting beads
and silent by the lake.

What is it that they hope to find
in silence? God speaking
in a pheasant's cry? Some
windy message? The sound of wheat
growing for their holy bread?

Don't they know how noisy faces are?
How grasshoppers chatter
at the corner of your eye?
Weeds work up over nothing,
and there is talk of years
in the cracking of your bones.

I thought in the Bible
God spoke with a voice.
Around here, children
marking dirty words
on the playground curb
are the only fingers
writing on stone.

## 33. FATHER TRACY

They make headcheese
and blood sausage here,
pickle the feet of pigs.

Smoked tongue, cracklings
from the rendered fat,
a slow boil for the heart.

## 34. DELBERT

In the slough
toadstools so small
are blood red pins
keep the logs
held down.

I wade.
Nothing holds the sky.
Why is evening deep
so deep?

## 35. CLARA

They will call her child a name.

It will rise out of the blacktop
or float like milkweed in a vacant lot.
Moving mouths once rose that way
when I tagged my brother to the playground
at four and five, when I followed
with a penny for a treat.

*Shadow, shadow*
their throats would call
though it was nothing I understood.

*Shadow*
and they'd leap from swings
stomping the outline
the sun threw as my twin.

*Shadow*
and I'd quickly turn
to find them trailing,
loose-shouldered as apes
with fingers on their lips.

*Shadow*
and I'd shrink behind
the corner of the school,
forgetting that my silhouette
stretched and would protrude.

*Shadow, Shadow*
and the morning sun grew thin.
Every time I saw those hollow mouths,
it was spring or summer and from the lake
a January wind.

## 36. SISTER JOAN OF ARC

In winter
this country
is all black and white.

Shadows take over.
Farmers wear frost
like a day-old beard

and the body curves
into the chill—
a black shape honed

to plow white air.
There is peace
in such clarity.

Fences draw lines
on the empty field—
a melodic staff

of clear, quiet notes.
Memory levels;
furrows grow pale.

But driving to New Ulm,
snow shimmies
across the road:

a scarf of a different color—
a belly-dancer's veil.

## 37. ELISE

I think I am becoming a cat.

Tongues of laziness
lick the slow stretching
of my afternoons.
When I stroke

my body, an engine purrs.
My eyes see more
when the lids are lower;

my knees are sleepy now.
My belly-button squints
a little less each day.

## 38. DELBERT

In Rusty Nail tavern,
they shake words to laughing
like beer you pour too fast
makes foam.

Some words
they only say
with spitting.

But nobody calls
my sister
a bitch!

## 39. ELISE

He has one black eye
and what the police report
(which Pa must never see)
calls "numerous abrasions."
He says he fell out of the truck.
Who would have thought
he'd fight for me?
All those angry years
as though my birth
had snatched his Ma away
then stole the sky
that wrapped around
his silent hunger.

Somehow I have gotten in,
the way those words,
even when his back was turned,
slid down the bar
and slipped along the wires
to his brain.

Del, what do you call
an explosion caused by a name?
a dam that breaks over barroom laughs?
a cellar stored with harvests
I thought could not exist?
All my life you have stared
through a kind of lidless dark.

Del, give me a word for this.

## 40.  SISTER JOAN OF ARC

I made a pact with God,
but the mistake, I think,
was in the bartering.

Here on the prairie,
they do not bargain with the sky.
Good crops are the usual forecast,
occasional hail, a remembered summer
of locusts, dust storms
if you plow foolishly, sudden gales.
Winter keeps you prudent,
outlines what you have built,
moves you closer in fewer rooms.
The rain is read as good.

I made a pact because
I wanted to be safe
from the elements:
from heat, from icy sorrow,
from the white blizzard
of having sinned.

If I leave now
I go alone on a prairie of uncut grass,
mapless and poorly equipped.
But this time I am saying:
I will not bribe You.
There is still a pact,
but terms are different now.

You owe me nothing.
Whatever comes is gift.

## 41. FATHER TRACY

Again
that girl's in my dreams.

Last night
I was rowing on the lake
and she was treading water
just beyond my reach;
her hands made words—
keeping her afloat.

She made a word
I somehow knew meant "peace."
I swear it was a heron,
wings spread and lifting off.

## 42.  ELISE

i

I could tell them *why*
but no one asks.
It was the window of the wolf.

In a taxidermist's shop,
when winter lost me
on a fieldtrip to St. Paul,
a white wolf in a quick white glance
drew me through the glass.

I had seen death before:
pullets drowned to blueness
in a storm, steers stunned
for the butcher's axe.
This was the moment before.

This was the snarl that freezes
on the lip, eyes iced
green and sharp. The terror
of a tunnel like a throat
open too deep to tell
if screaming makes a noise. This
is what the hearing know:
silence is the second
beyond the last sound.

So I laughed when his lips
made words he thought were love
in the truck-stop booth. I slid
my hands around his own throat's laugh,
felt them whisper along the limbs,
talking us into the dark.

His hands groped, but not for words,
and what he signed on my body
was a language so urgent
no woman has needed to learn.

I did not take him in ignorance.
I knew what tiny fish
swim in that spill
of pleasure. I caught one
that dived like a trout
to my deepest pool.
Fish, then fowl, now
it squirms like a pup,
grows hair and nails,
prepares to burrow out.

This child
will have a voice. Even before
they wipe the blood away,
it will know
the red tunnel leads to one of white.

Even before they cut it from me,
it will know
there is a wolf that waits
on the white edge of silence;
and against that frozen word,
this child will raise
a hot and lusty voice.

## 43. CLARA

*Our name lives now,*
Wilbur signed
when I bore him a daughter.

*Our name WILL live*
when I gave him a son.

He did not believe
in the body's resurrection;
so we wrapped him in wildflowers
and buried him like roots
his hands had pruned for the soil.

The children live, *will* live,
and some nights I wake
and know full well
he has not crawled under.
He waits like potatoes
in the cellar's darkest part.
The eyes are there,
tiny cores poised to open
the moment the first light breaks.

Next time, I tell him,
we will sprout up stronger.
We will live in a country
where even shadows have a voice.

## 44. ELISE

This child
will not want
for comfort in the night.

For better, for worse,
he is the son of this town,
and the whole town sleeps
with one eye open.

# A Breeze Called
# the Fremantle Doctor

Fremantle, Western Australia, 1864–1993

> *. . . a pleasant coolness in the heat,*
> *solace in the midst of woe . . .*
>
> Sequence for Pentecost
> STEPHEN LANGTON, 1228

*for Carole Walton, storyteller*

# Asylum 1864: Tess

*Out of Ireland have we come.*
*Great hatred, little room,*
*Maimed us at the start.*
*I carry from my mother's womb*
*A fanatic heart.*

W. B. YEATS

*In July of the past year, the lunatics, both Male and*
*Female, were removed from the old make-shift building to*
*the present well-built Asylum, a change from a low*
*swampy ground to a high, dry and airy site, from small,*
*ill-ventilated wards, from whence there was not the*
*slightest glimpse obtainable of the outside world . . . to a*
*pleasant overlook over land and sea.*

SURGEON GENERAL, WESTERN AUSTRALIA, 1864

## 1. Tess: Asylum

Even the swans are charry here,
black as hearth-pots, black
as the hair on my Jacky's head,
black as sins
that will send me sure
to burn in the fires of hell.

I am burning now,
though Father Neill never preached
so pale a fire, never said
an inch of sand
could hide a soil of flame,
a sun spark stones
as sure as any flint.

I am tinder,
and Jacky's dead, and those
who keep me here say I am not
a convict now. This
is asylum, but this
is what they do not know:
I am already gone.
I went up that night in Jacky's smoke,
rising above the billabong,
and what is here and penned
like sheep inside these limestone walls
leaves each afternoon
with the doctor-breeze,
floats to the east
with the ease of a lover.

I am gone, but I am not
in Connemara.

Jacky,
how did this come to be?

## 2. Tess: Theft

He had a taste for salmon,
my Jacky did, and I had a taste
for lips. Black-haired, the both of us,
like a wild wind, and never a fear
of warden's badge or father's belt
when the moon was right
for poaching what we wanted.

"That one'll not marry ye,"
my mother said, "a rover, he is,
not a kettle to his name
and carries himself like a bishop."

She'd have wed me to economy:
a flat board of a man,
gone gray in the neck,
saving his coppers twenty years
for a piece of bog, a hut
of stone, a chance
to pass his precious name on.

"Aye, you're the lass of dark rivers,"
my Jacky said, "but I've the rod
and the wee, wiggly fish,"
and I followed him down
to the water's edge, night
in the trees, and the ocean's smell
coming on strong from the west.

That we could be sent
on a convict ship
seemed not so ill a wind—

he for his salmon, I for butter
from the house where I served,
a loaf of bread, a petticoat with lace.

"Down under," Jacky said that night
and pressed against the petticoat.
"And haven't I been longing to taste
those sweets below the belt of earth?"

## 3. Tess: Transport

The salmon was not my Jacky's first,
and there was spring lamb
in the bargain. "A vagrant rogue"
is what my mother said, him transported
seven years to Botany Bay,
sailing on the *Rowena*. I sank

deep in the pits of a Galway gaol,
three months at hard labor
for my pilfered petticoat,
hoeing stinking potato hills,
while Jacky's wee fish
swam in my gut
mornings I puked the mash
and cabbage water. *Strumpet,*
my mother said, *no man*
*will look at ye,* and though I bled
the wee fish out—there in the rows
with the seaweed drying—
her door was already dark.

Sell or steal, I thought,
second time's the charm.
When the west winds rose
and the gaol door opened,
I found I had a taste for transport.

I stole my way to Dublin.

## 4. Tess: Passage

I went to Sydney, but I went free,
loaded on ship as "assisted" baggage—
a cargo of women to tame the men
whose tickets-of-leave were due,
who could finish their sentence
in the arms of a wife,
hire out for board and wages.

*Can churn and spin,*
the First Mate wrote,
*tend geese and wait on table.*

But other words sailed
when the ship left land:
*a flash piece of mutton, that one is!*
*a ewe, a hole, a sheila.*

Voices learned my name,
hands my waist, legs
blocked the passageways,
and every tongue the same:

> *Come on, Love, let's don't be shy.*
> *There's rum and sweets*
> *in the lifeboat tarp;*
> *there's the odd bit of lace*
> *stowed in my cabin.*

## 5. Tess: Equator

When we crossed the Line,
the sailors had their fun with us,
made a salty tub from an extra sail
and dunked us one by one,
our faces smeared with pitch.

Pay or be dunked, a rule of the sea,
one of those girdles no one can cross
without a drench or a forfeit.

I had already paid,
swimming in vomit when the squalls
came up, the hatches down,
trading the day for nightmare.

Oh, I saw the ghost—
her a Dublin whore who leaped
when her second one died,
their wee throats raw as porpoise meat
carved on deck, the milk of their skin
suckling yellow leeches. Ten days
and she was back again, walking the deck
the night the Mallon boy bit
clear through his tongue, the night
old Mercy Flanner crossed her path
and fell in fright down a hatchway.

My ghost is small—
a ruddy clot in a potato row,
a passage halfway to the altar.

Jacky, I have been true.
That line I have not crossed.

## 6. Tess: Landfall

Something black
is living in my head. Something spins
that makes me lose all sense
of where I'm bound for. Last night,
I left the room in the kitchen shed
where I'm to live, walked to rocks
below the mountain's shelf.

I heard a dog they call a *dingo* howl.
I heard parrots natter in the trees.
I heard again the hoots of stringy men
who lined the quay to choose
a bride, a brood mare, a willing sow
as we paraded down the gangway.

Black heads in plenty turned,
and many eyes were wild,
but none had Jacky's face,
none had my Jacky's smile.

> *A bloke transported October last?*
> *Not here, my girl! New South Wales*
> *is done with transport.*

> *If your mate's a con, he's in the West—*
> *dredging the Swan or*
> *breaking rock in Fremantle's port.*
> *Best find yourself employment.*

Could I be walking there, I said?
Might a cart soon be going?

> *Could you walk to China, lass?*
> *Could you cross sand the likes of the ocean?*

136

### 7. Tess: Parramatta Gaol

I am not "daft."
I am not "the sweepings of the parish."
I came here free, good as the bitches
who trot the town on a husband's arm,
whisper of *the Irish* over their tea:
*Their drink, my dear, their depravity* . . .

"Assisted" does not mean slave.
For two years, I made their beds,
rubbed floors with sand,
emptied their dainty pisspots,
and got me scarce a penny more
above a convict's wages.

Now I am not free. A silver cruet
in the bottom of my tucker-bag
waltzed me not to Jacky,
but to Parramatta Gaol. Now
I am torched by sun, rubbed raw
by sorting daggy wool, rotting
in the smell of women leaking
the seed of guards who want
their penny's worth of pleasure.

And: I am confined by dreams.

### 8. Tess: Western Australia

Today, I am set sail again,
not a possession, but not yet free,
assigned ticket-of-leave
to the only man going west,
Mr. Joseph Collier, Esq.,
a wombat-headed drone
who fancies himself a farmer.

I fancy waking to the kookaburra's hymn—
Jacky's laughter in a kingfisher's throat.
I fancy meeting him by a billabong
when the evening's calm,
and him out swaggering—
      a bushranger escaped from gaol,
      a crack stockman on a saddle horse,
      a miner come from the goldfields
      to claim me as his own.

I fancy he'll be saying
fairies dance on my shoulders
in blue gowns and green.
I fancy good omens
when we set sail:
red skies at night
and magpies for joy.
But last night on shore,
something blacker
flew from the dusty gums
and circled round me thrice:
three huge and haughty cockatoos,
black as night with a yellow crown,
black as sea without a moon, black
as my poor Jacky's hair.

## 9. Tess: Swan River Basin

I was born of clay, but I live in flame.

Three years of singeing at Parramatta,
my skin going dark, my lungs igniting,
my handkerchiefs blooming red flame;
now this:

fire, fire, and all of it male,
the blackboys going up,
their flower stalk rising
like a member inflamed,
the banksia already orange, already
burning as I burn each night
he comes to my shack: *the wife,*
*she's sick again, and well,*
*we wouldn't want more reports*
*that silver's up and missing. . .*

Fire in the blackboys,
fire between my legs,
the natives burning fields
to flush out kangaroos,
to cleanse the land, to crack
the seedpods too tough to crack
in air or rain or wind.

Some nights I see visions in the ash;
I see cities in the embers:
I see the bloody clot in the potato row
transformed by heat and sand.

"Be still," I tell it. "Be patient.
Our time will come."
Since they took my Jacky away,
everything is flame.

## 10. Tess: Wake

The crows are black, sooty-winged,
and they hang in the trees
outside the hut
where my Jacky is laid,
death, death in the trees,
though no one sung him with a bone
as the blackfellas do;
he sung himself, my Jacky did,
died for a salmon and a wild night,
and I the blessed cause of it.

Neighbors ride for miles to say
that this is Mr. Collier dead,
felled by a horse and a cobra snake,
but I've been burned past snakebite,
and I see what others don't.

This is Jacky come back
in Mr. Collier's face—
back from bushranging,
back from the goldfields,
back from burrowing out
of the Fremantle gaol.

All night, the blackfellas sing
across the billabong, the neighbors say
Collier was a "fair-dinkum mate,"
pass his whiskey and then
stand in the doorway to piss it out.

I bide my time, raise the jug
till my gullet catches blaze,
do then what the blackfellas do:
I cleanse, I purify, I tip the lamp
into the thatch and laugh
to see it all go up, the jug spilled,
the neighbors waking to flame,
the shell of gumwood cracking
to let the spirit out.

Hands grab and say that I am mad.
They pull me into a wide-starred night,
beat out the hem of my skirt,
say I could have killed myself
could have killed us, all and each.

That is wrong. They do not see
I can no longer be killed
by fire. I am a blackboy stem,
a gumnut riding flame, and Jacky,
Jacky, I have set you free.

## 11.  Tess: Fremantle Asylum: Extreme Unction

The man at my bed
is a black, black swan,
a charred sheep
collared in white,
and I without a shepherd,
I without a staff or crook
to catch the words
that frisk like lambs
around the borders
that are not yet burned.

*Several days now,*
Nurse Tillet says,
*always quiets down*
*evenings with the breeze...*
*The lungs are too far gone,* she says,
*God rest her soul...*
And something mumbles at my feet.

*Jesus Christus,* it says,
an old language colored green:
Connemara, sheep at rest,
hills above the sea...
*Ego te absolvo,* it says,
and in the gloaming, my mother
is kneeling at her beads.

A hand glides to my lips now,
now to my brow. The oil
tastes sweet, the scent
is thyme, but this is not

my Jacky's hand,
this is the charred sheep's,
and he seems so sad
I want to tell him
I am not convicted now,
I am already free.

*Et in aeternum,*
the green words say,
*Et in aeternum,*

and Jacky, my Jacky
comes from the western sea.

# Asylum 1883–1916: Margaret

*Whether I was truly in Australia at all,*
*or whether in the body or out of the body—*
*I cannot tell; but I have had bad dreams.*

JOHN MITCHEL

*Increase in population brings with it an increase in lunacy.*

SURGEON SUPERINTENDENT BARNETT, 1886

## 1. Margaret: Commitment

I did not try to kill the baby.
No matter what he said,
no matter what they wrote
in that leather-bound book,
that record of wildness,
its pages restrained
like the lunatics
whose names went down
spider after inky spider,
scrambling to escape the page.

I know what they wrote.
I know what my husband told them,
standing there wringing his hat
like a pullet's neck.
"Can we eat that?" I said.
"Can we eat that like the chickens
that were going to scratch, scratch
in the bloody red dirt and make us
a blooming fortune?"

"She says things that don't make sense,"
he said. "Sometimes she don't talk at all.
It's too much for me," he said,
"too much for all the little ones,
for Gemma, first of the lot
and her just after turning twelve."

Let him say what he wants;
I did not leave the baby to die.
I left it to live, live
but somewhere else,
to become a goanna,
changing colors as it moves,
to become a quick lizard
becoming one with the sand.

## 2. Margaret: Confinement

They have made us into chickens
penned in the glare of an afternoon,
our white dresses smoothed by hands
that roam and roam
with nowhere to perch,
our combs of red sorrow
our wattles of rage
clipped, clipped
like wings, like the shadow
we cannot escape
in this cloister of a courtyard.

"You'll be peaceful here,"
he said, but that's a laugh.
What kind of peace
can limestone give
when every step rattles
old bones of jarrah wood,
and there's nothing in your arms
but the ghost of a baby
you did not kill,
and it lived, lived,
though nothing lives here
but the ghosts of chickens,
*chooks* they say,
cackle, cackle, all day long,
the face you had
gone to nothing now,
pale as limestone
splattered with sun,
and asylum is a bit of shade,
a bit of green, a sail

in the purple river of sunset,
the green river of blood
that courses through
the back of hands that will not,
will not be still.

### 3.  Margaret: Lessons

They did it in Cornwall.
I know this for truth:
put the newborn babe
on the new tilled earth,
on nights of no or little moon.
I suppose it cried; I suppose
it was cold, but exposure
was brief, and better to know
which direction earth pulls,
how little space abides
between the waters of the womb
and the land's soggy maw.

I put mine in a cave of rock,
red-rimmed, boulder-strewn.
I planned to nurse it
evenings, mornings, noons,
to let it try to affix itself,
as I can never be affixed
to a soil not soil, but sand.

I wanted to harden it,
as soap must harden
to be more than fat and lye,
to season it
as new pots are taught
to be separate from food.
I would have watched

its color change
with each new sky;
I would have told it
that in empty land
no loneliness
is deeper than a mother's.

## 4. Margaret: Wind

All the chooks work in the laundry shed
where the cauldron heats, and the lye—
the lie—that we cleanse men's clothes
comes clean when we cannot cleanse
our own souls, our own bodies
of the hot spume men leave in us,
as the cattle leave dust—not steaming
cowpats here, but turds, dry turds
that give birth to flies that stick
to eyes, to nose, till every bit of excrement,
even the childrens' left behind a bush,
is alive, alive, moving and creeping forward,
closer to sand, to dust, to which
we are destined to return,

and returning once from Geraldton,
we stopped on a shore of such
white sand I thought I saw snow
there in the heat, in the dryness,
in the sand around the Pinnacles,
those spires of rock,
so late in the moon
I thought they were standing stones,
runes the Old Ones erected,
but they told me no, no,
the blackfellas never erected these
—only wind and waves and thousands
of years—or Kangaroo-man and
Wallaby-man in the darkness
of the Dreamtime,

but *all* here is dream, a fever of time
that never was, a view of hell
in an ice-blue sea, and if only
I did not have to catch
so many little souls
and turn them into bodies, as I
have done seven times, though two
are dead, and this one, this one
I planned to keep pale, to keep
from leathering, as we used to keep
cream in the springhouse so it was
cool, cool

as a body can be, but I
do not have a body,
I have melted from heat, from
the colors of childbirth
all run together, and I

I have become a wind.

## 5. Margaret: Jackeroo

I was not always made of air.
In Devon, I was an earthly lass,
but earth shifted, and I
had to cross when my mother crossed—
she to her just reward, I to Wooloona,
Aunt Ada and a cooking shack,
on sheep land west of Melbourne.

I met my husband in the evening shade—
I watering the little pippin trees
come from Cornwall
with their promise of fruit,
he, a green hand but older,
smelling of sheep-dip, the oil
of fleeces he could not yet shear.
I thought that we were suited—
I, the orphan, and he, the jackeroo—
were new, fresh, green
as the countries we left behind,
eager as border collies.

Eagerness is not enough,
and the land back-of-beyond
is always there tempting.
We moved as labor to a hill farm,
a cattle station, a godforsaken
chunk of dirt where he
attempted raising pigs. Then
he heard of the goldfields,
then of free land in the far,
far west.

Each move
I carried another child. Each move
I tried to leave behind regret.

## 6. Margaret: Conception

Blackfella women "catch" their babies
from the Dreamtime beasts, snag
a wallaby-spirit in wallaby land,
a honey-bee child in a space that's sweet.

Black Maisie told me this,
working in the dairy shed, days
she didn't have the urge
to go walkabout, to dig turtle eggs,
to sneak my soap down to the billabong
and make bubbles for her kangaroo boy,
her goanna girl, sudsing up
the little our cattle had to drink.

"Babies come from men," I told her,
"from the brine they leave inside."

"You funny missus," Maisie said.
"Men in you *all* time.
Bad time come—no baby.
Food no good—no baby.
Baby, him suck—no new baby.
Spirit angry—no baby to catch."

Then why did I catch so many? And worse:
why did I love them each? Why take
to my breast bodies slippery from birth
and feel myself plunge into warmth
so vast, an ocean so deep

I thought I could never feel rain,
never know again the presence
of unrelenting heat?

What did that lightness drain from me?
How does a desert continue to bloom?

## 7. Margaret: Cave

When Chester died in Victoria,
my first and green-eyed boy,
I buried him next to Aunt Ada's cross
on a wee and windy hill.
When Nellie blazed here,
fever shooting through her like a star,
there was scarce enough wood
for the little box, no flower
but the bottle-brush, no place
on the vast escarpment
for her to nestle in.

I have never nestled. Five months gone
with my seventh one, I made
my own shade, began to roam
toward Nellie's grave, toward dusk,
toward a little snuggery of acacia bush
fronting a boulder-spill—giant loaves
lurched from a red-orange soil,
pumpkins dropped from a cosmic cart.

One eve, Black Maisie stood
in the shadow of the boulders.
"Woman place. Secret," she said,
pointing through the acacia bush.
"Much dreaming. Much strong. Old."
She looked at my belly, swollen
already with this year's catch.
"Girl baby," she said, "Honey bee,"
and she held the branches
as I ducked behind her, stood in eerie light
beneath an overhang of presences

faded but aglow: large, mouthless heads,
haloes of ochre rays, stick-women
with winnowing bowls, handprints
stenciled by a spray of white.

I reasoned how this should go:
I would bring indigo or ink,
trace the baby's fingers,
her little palm, know
she could belong to this place,
her breath part of the dreaming,
her hands part of the stone.

## 8. Margaret: Violation

I told him
I felt peaceful within the rock;
I contained an inner breeze.
I told him women's blood
disappears, month by month,
red earth by earth, and we
must draw our palm-prints
onto sacred stone to stay. I told him
the child was safe, the deed
was done, but he dragged me
from the house, forced me
to straddle the horse
ahead of him.

       I told him
the cave was women-space,
forbidden, it's power bad
for men, but he slapped me
into the acacia bush, grabbed
the child, and with a stone
raked across the palm-print,
slashed the women with winnowing bowls,
ground out the auras of yellow light,
the faces watchful and old.

I told him
I was no longer his wife.
I told him he had killed the baby's soul.
I told him I would walk not ride,
and I did not go home.

## 9. Margaret: Corroboree

And then I descended into darkness.
I became black, and I walked
beyond myself into a space
back of the billabong
where native fires burned
and the blackfellas painted
not stone but self
in great swaths of white—
white dots big as smallpox, white
diamonds, white squares. Aprons
of eucalypt covered their privates,
ruffs of gum leaves shook
their ankles into storm.

Women beat time on possum skins;
men clacked sticks seared in flame.
A didgeridoo hollowed the air
and singing carved the night.
I do not know what cause
they had to celebrate, why
young men seemed to split
themselves, their legs quivering
closer and closer to the ground,
their bodies a trunk, a tree
in which the smallest birds
could come to rest.

I split too, and when
the dancing was done,
I pulled the dawn around me;
I became a dream
as I have since become the wind.

### 10. Margaret, 1916:

### The Fremantle Residence
### for Poor Ladies

I am not a lunatic now.
Thirty years onward,
I have been renamed,
reclassified, left here
as indigent, aged,
harmless even to the self,
the other lunatics gone,
packed and shipped
to a new coop up in Claremont.

I do not really need a name.
I ride easy in the light
of morning, afternoon, schooled
to need nothing and therefore
be rich. From the garden
I see ships in the harbor; I hear
a parrot above me, its cry
counting the skies: *eighty-six,*
*eighty-six, eighty-six.*

I no longer count what happens,
and I do not know
where my children live.
Some nights before sleep,
the velvet of small bodies
lies next to mine,
but to remember is to dream,
and to dream is to gather
the thinnest threads that memory spins
and twine them into songs

to map the road you'll travel by.
And, to enter the *Dreaming,*
as Maisie well knew,
is to sing outside of time,
to dream outside of sleep,
to let the spirit know at last the truth:

there is no difference
between the body and the breeze.

# Asylum 1993: Sonia

*I love a sunburnt country . . . a wilful, lavish land . . .*

Dorothea MacKellar

*When you set out for Ithaka*
*Pray that your road's a long one . . .*

C. P. Cavafy

## 1. Sonia: House Call

That first night the Doctor came
when I had abandoned hope
of sleep; everything strange—
a reversed hemisphere—
January heat cooped up
in my empty flat, the air
a hundred and four
when I deplaned.

High above Fremantle's piers,
its convoluted streets, I unpacked,
bathed, went from bed
to chair, to cushions tossed
on a tile floor, wondered
if heat stroke and jet lag
could cause a heart attack,
my body aflame, my asthma up.
Then, the gentleman caller,
the Doctor, came,
sweeping through my windows
and luring me to bed.

New friends would argue
the etymology: *doctor*
or *docker*, a healing hand
or a windy push into port,
but does it matter which?
I've brought wounds enough
for months of therapy,
and like any woman
awash in a bed,
I dream of arriving
again and again.

## 2. Sonia: Foreign Travel

In strange countries,
you learn to walk differently,
your stride curbed by open gutters,
your arch rounding cobblestones.

Here, I learn to be languid,
to slow until my movement
is but a little break in air.
Mornings, I close the flat,
draw curtains, exile the day
to an air-cooled office, wait
until the Doctor calls again.

In the great void of Sunday,
church and cappuccino done,
I seek asylum where I can find it:
cinemas, bookstores,
this garden cloistered deep
in limestone shade.

"Lunatics" once walked here,
laundered their visions
in the outer courtyard,
hung their fractured songs
on walls their silence made.

I am not so different from them.
Heat, malaise, aloneness
are countries on a border;
the mind crosses into shadow
when it can move no more
to create a healing shade.

## 3. Sonia: Dark Sunday

. . . and so I'm stuck here, she says,
godforsaken country built on nothing
but sand, nothing but dust, endless
gray-green eucalypts, and he,
*he*, up in some toffy house in Claremont,
the new wife, *if* she's that, blonde
of course, and thirty, and how can I
get back to Leicester when even a crack
steno job barely pays the rates, but he
had to emigrate: *opportunity*, and
*our one chance*, and did he think
how I'd fare here, my hip worse,
worse than Leicester, never mind
that business of dry, salt air,
there's mold here, rising damp
from basements, foundations, the whole
esplanade reclaimed from the sea,
and sunshine too is different here,
the skies a brutal blue, and no
ozone anymore, the Red Cross
with sunscreen in two-litre jugs,
admitting we live in a cosmic hole,
and why

are *you* here? she says.

Students, I say,
a chance to teach abroad.
I do not say: *I sleep each night*

*to reconfigured stars, I wake*
*as morning strikes the sea like flint.*

Adventure, nosiness, I say,
and she cannot hear me chanting:
*the light, the light, the light...*

## 4. Sonia: Totems

i

My friend Judith says
the blackbird entered the room,
circled the black man thrice,
its wings a heavy cursive
writing on the afternoon.
He knew that airy alphabet:

*Someone you love has died.*

ii

Aboriginals do not eat
the flesh of spirit kin—
the soul their mothers caught—
(wallaby-boy, cockatoo-girl),
brother, sister, incarnate
of rock, of dream, of air.
I think of fish on Friday,
dietary laws, the usual breakfast
of Sunday morn:

*This is my body ... This
my blood ...*

iii

In the outdoor opera,
Dreamtime spirits come on stilts.
Lofty and clothed like sky,

171

they enter earth's domain—
the russet, the ocre, the char
of mortals and their bits
of dress. Before us,
fires burn, sun and moon
create themselves, ascend
to the tale every culture tells:

how lofty the stars, how
endless our aspiring.


      iv

One swarthy midnight,
I rose from bed, and from
my stuccoed fourth-floor balcony,
I watched a man and woman
noiselessly strip, noiselessly slip
into the blue ether of
the swimming pool below.

I saw their fur glisten
in the moonlight. I saw
their heads break the surface,
sleek seals moving
toward the undertow.


      v

I've had lorikeets on my shoulder,
have fed a tender joey who

took my hand in both of his.
I've seen a red-back spider,
most fatal of widows,
clinging to a plastic pail
in a noonday courtyard ditch.

One dusk I watched
an injured kangaroo
wheeling like a drunk,
a Charlie Chaplin of marsupials,
each hop a silent riff.

And, at Margaret River,
sick and coughing in a tent,
I woke to rain and kookaburras:
an eerie human laugh,
the season beginning to shift.


vi

I leave not knowing
which is the inner animal:
the shadow dolphin
longing for the surf,
the dingo, the hooded lizard,
the singer of song-lines,
the woman not yet willing
to loose her hold on earth.

## 5. Sonia: After/Word: Indiana

Longing for the light
persists. In that other country,
that dream-clad edge of sea
stretching back to India,
even the limestone walls
fed back the brightness,
even the dullest of trees
startled into bushy blooms—
the banksia erect,
the stamens of the bottle-brush
a spun galaxy of red.

Some mornings a rooster
not yet broken to urban life
saluted those hills of sand,
and sometimes I walked
the streets of that town
alight with gladness, as though
I had already crossed the border
where only light exists.

Words came back: *amo,
amas, amat,* that old conjugation,
and I wondered if the verb
could be objectless, intransitive.
I wondered how it came to be
that past the middle of my life,
I walked alone in brazen light
and parsed the words for love.

# Glossary of Australian Terms[*]

*banksia:*  a shrub that produces a rigid orange bloom that looks rather like a corn-dog

*blackboy:*  a low tree that is able to survive brushfires and continue to live and grow with a blackened trunk

*blackfella:*  an aboriginal person

*billabong:*  a watering hole

*Botany Bay:*  an area near Sydney where many convict ships landed. It was so called because botanical specimens were gathered there by earlier expeditions. The name became synonymous with convict exile.

*bushranger:*  an outlaw who robs travelers or isolated homesteads in the bush

*chook:*  slang for chicken

---

[*]Aboriginals on the vast continent of Australia have many language groups. The words given here are those which have come into common usage among Australians.

*corroboree:* an aboriginal gathering usually including singing and dancing and sometimes sacred traditional rites

*didgeridoo:* an aboriginal wind instrument often made from a hollow tree branch or root. It makes a low and eerie sound.

*dingo:* a wild desert dog

*Dreamtime (or dreaming):* the ancient time of creation in aboriginal mythology. Sacred animals, whose spirits continue into the present, created the world and established a kind of natural law and ritual. Many aboriginal groups make little distinction between memory and dream since both deal with events, persons or objects which are not physically present. Hence, the Dreamtime is also a history.

*fair-dinkum mate:* a term of approval applied to a loyal and trusted friend.

*goanna:* a large lizard able to camouflage itself. It is eaten by aboriginals still living on the land.

*jackeroo:* an inexperienced sheep hand

*joey:* a baby kangaroo

*kookaburra:* a bird related to the kingfisher. Its call sounds like a prolonged and raucous human laugh.

*lorikeet:* a small, brilliantly colored parrot

*Parramatta:* a town near Sydney that housed an infamous female prison during the convict era.

| | |
|---|---|
| *sheila:* | an often demeaning term for a woman. Americans might say "babe" or "chick." |
| *sung with a bone:* | the aboriginal equivalent of putting a curse on someone which will cause that person's death |
| *ticket-of-leave:* | a permit allowing a convict to go to work before serving a complete sentence. Similar to parole. |
| *toffy:* | high-class, snooty, or showy |
| *transport:* | the term used for transportation to Australia as a criminal sentence |
| *tucker:* | food |
| *walkabout:* | an aboriginal practice, sometimes associated with maturation rituals, of self-sufficient wandering |
| *wombat:* | a dark-furred marsupial about the size of a badger |